Teaching scientific enquiry

CW00607369

Booster Book
for Key Stage 1

Lawrie Ryan
Rosemary Sherrington

Published in 2002 by:
Nelson Thornes Ltd
Delta Place
27 Bath Road
CHELTENHAM
GL53 7TH
United Kingdom

02 03 04 05 06/ 10 9 8 7 6 5 4 3 2 1

A catalogue record for this book is available from the British Library

ISBN 0 7487 6868 8

Illustrations by Oxford Designers & Illustrators
Page make-up by Oxford Designers & Illustrators

Printed in Great Britain by Ashford Colour Press

Contents

Introduction

Science Attainment Target 1 (Sc1) is the most important aspect of science at Key Stage 1. It is here that the foundations will be set for the rest of a child's science education. The 'hands-on' experiences provided for children will help develop their understanding of the world, and give them the skills to become increasingly independent investigators.

This book offers teachers a flexible resource that can be used to develop skills at different levels in a range of common enquiries tackled throughout Key Stage 1. The enquiries all feature in the QCA Scheme of Work, but extra guidance, especially with differentiation, is included in the notes for teachers that accompany each activity. The enquiries are arranged in the order they appear in the QCA Scheme of Work.

Nelson Thornes *Primary Science Kit*, *Blueprints: Science Skills* and the *Teaching Scientific Enquiry CD-ROM* also provide useful support for your delivery of Sc1.

What's in the book?

A. Teacher's notes

Learning objectives

The learning objectives for each activity are listed at the start of an enquiry. The key features of those related to Sc1 skills are highlighted.

Lesson notes

These start with an approximate timing for the enquiry and define the type of enquiry the children will carry out. Based on work done by the AKSIS (ASE and Kings College Science Investigations in Schools) project, they can be designated:

- Fair tests (in which children change one factor, or variable, whilst keeping others the same)

- Biological enquiries (in which some factors are difficult to control, but the aim is to spot patterns: sample sizes are an important feature of these enquiries)

- Exploration (in which children can use their senses to observe things, sometimes over an extended period of time)

- Classification (in which children sort things into groups or identify things)

- Problem solving (in which children design solutions to a variety of problems, often technological)

- Research (in which children will consult secondary sources to answer their scientific questions)

This is followed by some outline suggestions for the lesson under the general headings:

- Introduction
- Group work
- Whole class

Differentiated Sc1 learning outcomes

Learning outcomes are the key to accurate assessment, and with each enquiry you will find learning outcomes at a variety of levels.

The differentiated sheets

A brief outline of each sheet is given and a star system is used to give a quick guide to differentiation (★ sheets offer most support and ★★★ sheets provide most challenge). Levels are indicated where sheets closely match a Level Description from Sc1.

Background information

Information for teachers is provided on the skills developed in the enquiry and on the science upon which the activity is based.

B. Sc1 Sheets

There are three types of sheet to go with each enquiry:

Skill development practice sheets

These give children an opportunity to practise a skill developed in the enquiry. These can be done before the enquiry to help prepare children for their activity. Alternatively, they can be used retrospectively in the light of diagnostic assessment information gained as children tackle their enquiry.

Differentiated Sc1 support sheets

These form the main body of the sheets and offer support at a variety of levels of demand and are to be used as children carry out their enquiry. The teacher can match sheets to different individuals or groups within the class.

Sc1 checklists

Children can use these sheets, with support, to record the aspects of the skill(s) they have performed in the course of their enquiry. Levels are included to aid teacher assessment of Sc1. These are based on the Level Descriptions whenever possible, but also include the authors' interpretation for finer differentiation.

Ourselves: How tall are we?

Nelson Thornes Ref: PS Kit 1.1.6

Learning objectives

Children should learn:

- to **ask questions and make suggestions** about growing and getting older
- to **make observations and comparisons** of height
- to **decide whether their prediction was correct**.

Lesson notes

 Approximate timing: 2 hours

Type of enquiry

This Sc1 enquiry will give children the opportunity to explore heights of children in their class. They have the chance to find out if there is a link between their ages and heights. This is an enquiry set in a biological context.

Introduction

Introduce the activity by asking the children about any differences they notice in heights between themselves and their friends. Encourage them to use appropriate language — taller than, shorter than, tallest, shortest, measure.

Ask them to compare each other's height. Stand with your friend, are you taller or shorter than they are?

Who in the class is taller/shorter than you?

Encourage them to ask questions about their height, and how tall they will grow — Will I grow as tall as …, taller than…?

Ask them if the oldest children are the tallest (yes, no, don't know).

How can we find out?

Group work

One way would be to line up the children in order of age, ask them about who they are standing next to and where they are in the line. Then take a photo. Next, line up in order of height, orient themselves and take a second photo. A digital camera will produce immediate results to look at.

Use standard height measurement where appropriate.

One non-standard way to measure and record children's heights is to use sheets of toilet tissue. In groups, the children measure each other, with help, to the nearest half sheet, put their name on the paper, count the number of sheets, and record it on a chart of names. Pin each length along the wall in order of height. Put the names into order of height. The children use Sheets 1 to 4 as appropriate.

Whole class

Stand the children in order of age facing the line of tissue, and let them compare their positions in the two lines. Discuss the differences and similarities.

Where are you on the line of height?

Who is next to you?

Who is the oldest/tallest? Who is the youngest/ smallest? Where are they in the line of tissue? Is it the same place in both lines?

Ask them whether the oldest are the tallest or the youngest the smallest. Reach an agreement about the conclusion drawn.

Ask about what they thought at first before they did the measurement.

Who thought at first, that the oldest would be the tallest? Who thought they would not? Who wasn't sure?

Reinforce the conclusion. What did we find out?

Differentiated Sc1 learning outcomes

Asking questions

- asks questions based on observations
- asks factual questions such as how big/tall?
- asks questions such as how, how much, how long, how tall?

Planning

makes suggestions:

- based on imagination — 'I'll grow as tall as a house'
- based on understanding — 'I'll grow to be as tall as my mum'
- based on understanding of the investigation — 'Let's measure everyone's height and see if the tallest are the oldest'.

Observing and comparing

- compares their height with a partner's
- compares the height of other children from observation
- compares the height of other children from line of tissues.

Deciding whether their prediction was correct (at the end of the investigation)

- remembers what they predicted
- says what they predicted
- increases their understanding in the light of evidence.

Using the differentiated sheets

Sheet 1★ is to give children practice in posing questions; in this case, by asking questions about an alien and a board game. Assistance is needed to listen to the children's questions. (Asking questions is an activity at all levels, but not specifically stated in the National Curriculum Level Descriptions.)

Sheet 2★ asks the children to make comparisons within their group. The group size should be 4–6. They will need help in answering the questions, which can be done orally. (Making comparisons is a Level 2 activity.)

Sheet 3★ asks the children to use a two-column table to draw themselves and their friend. They should indicate relative heights, i.e. that one is taller than/shorter than/the same height as the other. They could stand back to back and look in a mirror, or ask a third child to say who is taller. They will need help in answering the questions and this may be done orally. (Observation is a Level 1 activity and comparison is at Level 2.)

Sheet 4★★ asks the children to use a more precise comparison of heights, through measurement, with the data entered on a two-column table. This table may be used by children using the sheets of tissue (Level 2) or a standard method of measurement (Level 3).

Sheet 5 is a record of an individual child's achievements written in language they might use. At this stage, they will need help in completing these, or the teacher may prefer to complete it.

Background information

Asking questions

Usually, it is not difficult to encourage children to raise questions. Valuing all kinds of children's questions is important to children's learning; it is the way a child links experiences and makes their own sense of the world. Learning in science is helped, however, if teachers, and eventually pupils, distinguish between science-related questions and those that cannot be answered through scientific investigation. Questions that science is concerned with are about what there is in the world and how it behaves. 'Are the oldest children the tallest?' can be addressed by investigation, whereas 'Do you want to be tall when you grow up?' cannot be answered from observation and testing.

Note: In some homes, children are taught that it is rude to ask questions. This usually means questions of a personal nature, but many children do not see the difference. Tell them that it is not rude to ask questions about objects, or general things about ourselves, such as the tallest, the oldest, birthdays, likes and dislikes. Clarify the distinction between these and personal questions and remarks.

Observing

Observation of similarities, differences, changes over time and links between one feature and another are central to everyday learning. Observation and comparison are also pivotal to scientific work as starting points, during the course of an investigation and in drawing conclusions, such as analysing results. Observation plays a major part in doing investigations — exploring, watching changes over time, measuring and providing evidence for the linking of cause and effect.

In Key Stages 1 and 2 exploration and investigation are of everyday objects and events in familiar situations centred on themselves, the home, school and the immediate locality.

In this lesson the children are asked to find out if the oldest children are the tallest.

Help the children to compare their height with others' and the tallest with the oldest:

● Who is the tallest in the class?
● When is their birthday?
● Are they the oldest?
● Who else is tall?
● When is their birthday?
● Are they also one of the oldest?
● Are the tallest children the oldest?

Predicting

At first, it is not easy to help children to make genuine predictions rather than guesses or stating what they already know.

Questions such as these might help:

● What do you think will happen as you get older?
● Is everyone in the class the same height?
● Why do you think some of the children are taller than others?
● Do you think the youngest children are the smallest?
● Do you think the oldest children are the tallest?

Comparing predictions with results

By the end of a test, which may take an afternoon or more, many young children may have forgotten what they predicted. Faced with contradictory evidence, others may change their original idea. So much of learning is about being right or wrong, that this is entirely understandable. Take the children through carefully with questions such as:

● Can you remember what we were trying to find out?
● What did you think then?
● What do you think now we've done the measurements?
● Were you surprised?
● Did you change your mind?

and reinforce the process — it's good to change your mind if the test tells you different and does not support your original idea.

Name .... Date ....

Asking questions

(To do with the teacher or assistant.)

Here's an alien. It is friendly.
What would you like to know about it?

Think of some questions to ask.
(Write the questions here.)

....

....

....

(To do with the teacher or assistant.)

Here's a board game.

What questions could you ask
so that you can play it?

(Write the questions here.)

....

....

....

Name .... Date ....

How tall are we?

Draw the children in your group in order of height.

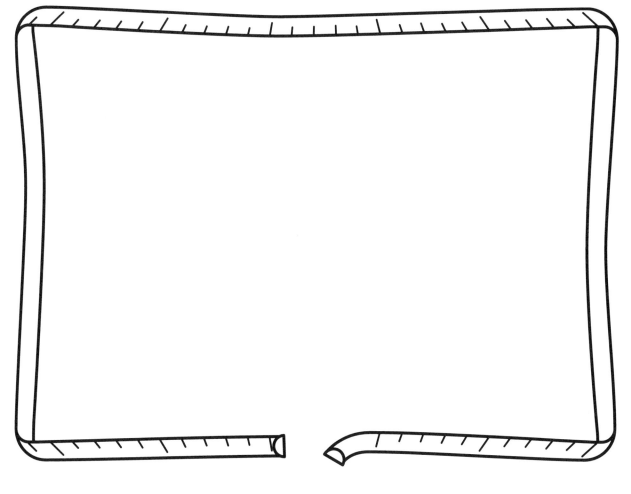

Who is the tallest? ....

Who is the shortest? ....

Who is the oldest? ....

Who is the youngest? ....

Is the tallest the oldest? ....

Is the shortest the youngest? ....

Name .... Date ....

How tall are we?

Draw yourself and your friend.

Name ....

Name ....

Who is taller? ....

Who is shorter? ....

How tall are you? ....

How tall is your friend? ....

Who is the tallest in the class? ....

Who is the oldest in the class? ....

Name .... Date ....

How tall are we?

Fill in the names and heights of the three tallest children in the class.

The tallest children	Height
....	....
....	....
....	....

Fill in the names and ages of the three oldest children in the class.

The oldest children	Age
....	....
....	....
....	....

Are the tallest children also the oldest? ....

Name .... Date ....

How tall are we?

Asking questions and making suggestions

❑ I asked a question about our heights.
(Level 1)

❑ I suggested how tall I would grow.
(Level 1/2)

❑ With some help, I suggested how to find out if the oldest children are the tallest ones.
(Level 2)

Making observations and comparisons

❑ With help, I can find differences in height between children in my class.
(Level 1)

❑ I can find differences in heights and ages between children in my class.
(Level 2)

Concluding

❑ I checked if my prediction was right or not.
(Level 2)

❑ We noticed that the oldest children are not always the tallest.
(Level 2)

Growing plants: Do plants need light to grow?

Nelson Thornes Ref: PS Kit 1.2.5

Learning objectives

Children should learn:

- that green plants need light to grow
- to **turn ideas** about whether green plants need light to grow **into a form that can be tested**
- to **observe and compare** green plants grown in light and dark places
- to **conclude** that green plants need light to grow well.

Lesson notes

 Approximate timing: 2 hours at intervals over two weeks

Type of enquiry

This Sc1 enquiry will give the children the opportunity to test whether plants need light to grow well. This is a biological enquiry.

Introduction

Introduce the activity by asking the children about plants and showing them several different green plants to establish their colour and variety. Include trays of 'cress' from greengrocers. Talk about light and the opposite — darkness.

Ask if plants need light to grow well (yes, no, don't know.)

Ask the children for ideas how to find out (choose dark and light places with similar conditions such as temperature).

Set up the investigation together. Set several small trays of seeds such as oilseed rape, grass or cress on a damp, absorbent surface such as towelling or several layers of kitchen paper. Put half in darkness, half in a light place, maintaining roughly the same temperature, and watering the trays as necessary. (It is better to set up a number of seeds rather than just one or two in case some do not germinate.)

Individual and group work

Help the children to observe the seedlings at intervals of, e.g. 3, 8 and 14 days.

Help the children to use Sheets 3, 4 and 5 as appropriate.

Whole class

Ask questions to find out the children's observations and comparisons.

- Did the plants grow better in light than in darkness?
- Do plants need light to grow well?
- Were any of you surprised by the results?
- Discuss their predictions.

Help the children complete Sheets 2, 3, 4 and 5.

Differentiated Sc1 learning outcomes

Turning ideas into a form that can be tested

● suggests growing some seeds
● suggests growing some seeds in light and some in dark conditions.

Observing and comparing

● finds differences between plants
● finds differences in how plants grow
● finds similarities in how plants grow
● notices changes in growing plants.

Concluding

● knows what they thought would happen
● compares their prediction with what happened
● learns that plants need light to grow well.

Using the differentiated sheets

Sheet 1★ is aimed at children getting used to comparing things; in this case, by marking differences and similarities with a cross. (Level 1)

Sheet 2★ is a skill sheet to provide an opportunity to draw a conclusion from the evidence presented in the pictures of the plants.

Sheet 3★★ asks the children to use a three-column table to record changes and differences in the seedlings over time. They will need help with recording any differences they notice. (The use of a simple table is a Level 2 skill.)

Sheet 4★★ asks the children to come to a conclusion about plants needing light to grow well from the evidence in the two drawings. (Saying whether what happened was or was not what they expected is a Level 2 skill.)

Sheet 5★★ is for higher attaining children to complete; if necessary, with help. Alternatively, it could be enlarged and used as the basis for a whole–class record of the activity.

Sheet 6 is a record of an individual child's achievements written in language they would use. The children will, at this stage, need help in completing these, or the teacher may prefer to complete it.

Background information

Planning

Making suggestions for a test is a very early stage of planning an investigation. Some children may suggest putting seeds to germinate in darkness (only). Ask them to think about the need to have others in light so that you can see the differences. Ask questions such as:

● If the seeds grow in darkness how will you know if they grow as well as/the same as they would in the light?
● Would it be better to put some in the light as well?
● Why?

The children will begin to consider the concept of fair testing later. For now, it is enough if the children can suggest that some seeds need to be put into a dark place and others into a light place.

Observing and comparing

Observation plays an important part in doing investigations — exploring, watching changes over time, measuring and providing evidence for the linking of cause and effect.

In this lesson the children are asked to look at the colour, shape, size of plants and changes in them over time, in order to answer the question: Do plants need light to grow well?

For learning to move forward, we need to know what the children think about plants.

One starting point could be to ask them to draw a plant to see what they include or leave out. In addition, ask obvious questions about a plant, such as:

● What are these?
● What can you see/do you notice?
● What colour/size/shape is it?
● What is it like?
● Where do you see/find them?

Include questions to encourage comparison:

● How are they different?

● How are they the same?

● Why do you think they are different?

● Have you noticed anything about the colour of all these plants?

Discuss and answer any questions the children ask.

Concluding or deciding what the results mean

Concluding involves putting bits of information or evidence together to make some statement of their combined meaning.

Two aspects of concluding are important in this activity:

● matching a prediction (was I surprised? was I right?)

● and reaching a conclusion (what have we found out from our test?).

This may be a process they are not aware of at this stage, although they will have intuitively reached many conclusions in the face of evidence during their lives.

Ask questions to take the children through the process:

● What did we do to the plants/seedlings that was different?

● What happened to the ones in the light?

● What happened to the ones in the dark?

● Which ones are strong, healthy and the right colour?

● What caused the other plants to be different?

● What have we found out from our test?

● How do you know this is right?

● Did you expect this to happen?

● Did you think that plants needed light to grow well?

● What have we found out from our test?

Plants and light

Plants need light to grow. They grow; that is, make new material from carbon dioxide and water, with light as the source of energy. The green colouring in plants is chlorophyll which absorbs sunlight. Oxygen is given off as a by-product. Plants usually continue to grow throughout their lives.

Name .... Date ....

Do plants need light to grow well?

Spot the difference

Put an X on 2 differences.

What is the same?

Put an X on 2 things that are the same.

Name .... Date ....

Do plants need light to grow well?

Concluding

In the light   **In the dark**

What do these pictures show? Tick the right answer.

❑ Plants need light to grow well.

❑ Plants need soil to grow well.

❑ Plants need water to grow well.

Name .... Date ....

Do plants need light to grow well?

Will plants grow well in the dark?

(Write yes or no.) ....

My results

	In light	**In dark**	**Difference**
3 days			
5 days			
8 days			

Name .... Date ....

Do plants need light to grow well?

Draw the seedlings in this box.

In the light	In the dark

What happened to the ones in the light?

....

What happened to the ones in the dark?

....

I said seeds in the dark would   ☐ grow well.
                                    ☐ not grow well.
                                    (tick one)

Were you right? ....

We found out that ....

Name .... Date ....

Do plants need light to grow well?

❑ I think plants need light to grow well.

❑ I think plants do not need light to grow well. (tick one)

We put some .... seeds onto .... and watered them.

We put them into a .... cupboard.

We put some more seeds onto .... and watered them.

We put these into a .... place.

Our results

After ...... days in the dark the seedlings were ....

....

In the light they were ....

After ...... days in the dark they were ....

In the light they were ....

After ...... days in the dark they were ....

In the light they were ....

What I learned

Plants need .... to grow well.

I know this because ....

....

Name .... Date ....

Do plants need light to grow well?

Making suggestions

❏ I suggested we put some seeds in the light and others in a dark place.
(Level 2)

Observing

❏ I noticed changes in the seedlings. (Level 1)

❏ I can find differences between plants. (Level 2)

❏ I can find differences in how plants grow. (Level 2)

❏ I can find similarities between plants. (Level 2)

❏ I can find similarities in how plants grow. (Level 2)

Concluding

❏ I know that the seedlings in the light were healthy and green and those in the dark were not so green and were straggly. (Level 2)

❏ I know that what happened was/was not what I expected. (Level 2)

❏ I found out that plants need light to grow well. (Level 2)

Sorting and using materials:
Magnetic or not?

Nelson Thornes Ref: PS Kit 1.3.5

Learning objectives

Children should learn:

● that some materials are magnetic but most are not
● to **predict** which objects they expect to be attracted to a magnet
● to **make observations**
● to **communicate what happened**
● to use results to **draw conclusions** saying whether their predictions were right.

Lesson notes

 Approximate timing: 1.5 hours

 Keep magnets away from computers and software.

Type of enquiry

This Sc1 enquiry will give children the opportunity to classify objects and/or materials as magnetic or not.

Introduction

Introduce the activity by asking children a few questions to gauge prior knowledge about magnets. For example:

● What are magnets like?
● What do they do?
● Who has played with a magnet before?
● What are they used for?

Show a couple of different magnets from everyday life, e.g. fridge magnets, magnet from a door/cupboard, magnet from a game. (Although fridge magnets are common in many kitchens, some children won't have seen them or will believe that they are made of plastic. If they have noticed the magnet itself, they might still think that it sticks to plastic because it is not obvious that a fridge is made of steel with a thin outer casing of plastic.)

Group work

Give the children time to explore a couple of magnets. Warn the children about the danger of damaging computer equipment with magnets. Let them 'play' for a few minutes. This gives some the chance to feel the 'magical' non-contact forces for the first time.

Then concentrate the groups on the task in hand — to group a selection of objects into two groups: magnetic and not magnetic. With magnets safely in the middle of the table, ask groups to predict which objects they think will be magnetic. They can record their predictions on Sheet 1 or 2. Sheet 6 is a combined prediction and results table.

The groups then test their predictions and record their results on Sheet 3 or Sheet 6. If time, let them test more objects and record the results themselves on Sheet 4.

Whole class

Ask groups to discuss what kind of things they found to be magnetic before the plenary, then review class results and draw conclusions. At this point Sheet 5 can be used to help sort out the objects.

Differentiated Sc1 learning outcomes

Predicting

- with help, predicts which objects will be attracted to the magnet
- predicts whether some objects will be attracted to the magnet (and records these in some way to refer back to after testing).

Observing

- observes each test as a separate event
- compares objects as magnetic or not magnetic as they test them.

Recording

- with help, can fill in charts provided
- fills in charts provided
- with help, can fill in tables provided
- fills in tables provided.

Concluding

- with help, checks correctly against predictions
- checks correctly against predictions
- sorts objects into groups of those that are magnetic and those that are not magnetic and checks correctly against predictions
- sorts objects into groups of those that are magnetic and those that are not magnetic, accepting that not all metals are magnetic, but iron is, and checks correctly against predictions.

Using the differentiated sheets

Sheet 1★ helps children get used to filling in charts, in this case by circling objects. (Level 1)

Sheets 2★★ and 3★★ use two-column tables to record simple yes/no predictions and results. (The use of a simple table is a Level 2 skill.)

Sheet 4★★ provides a blank table for children to choose their own objects to test.

Sheet 5★★ helps children record the sorting/ classifying exercise having completed their tests on the different objects. (Basic comparison between objects is a Level 2 skill.)

Sheet 6★★★ introduces more complex three-column tables. It can be used with children who are more confident in their writing skills. They can record their predictions and results in the same table. This is followed by the conclusion in which they check if their predictions were correct, and then construct a list of the magnetic objects tested. At this stage, the final conclusion will be that iron objects are magnetic.

Sheet 7 is the pupil record sheet to complete for this enquiry. The children will need help filling these in or teachers might wish to complete the sheet themselves.

Background information

Predicting

Most children will have played with magnets before, but they all need a chance to explore them again and remind themselves of what they can do. For example, they can find which part of a fridge magnet is the 'sticky' bit. Many will still make a 'guess', and others a prediction based on what they know already about the materials they have explored. Asking 'What makes you think this will stick to the magnet?' will help them to think about what they have discovered previously and help you discover which are predictions and which are guesses.

Making observations

It helps a great deal if the magnets used for the test are strong so that observations of whether a material is magnetic or not are very clear to the children. The magnet should pick up the object where possible, or 'stick' to it and make it move.

Communicating what happened

Talk to the children about what they found and ask them to show you what happened. This will enable them to use the correct vocabulary and check on their findings, discussing results with you and their partners.

Tables are ideal for recording which materials the children found to be magnetic.

Drawing conclusions and saying whether the predictions were right

Most of the children will be able to say which materials were attracted to a magnet. Encourage them to use their tables to talk about the results.

Questions such as these help children to make a generalisation:

● Which objects stuck to the magnet/did the magnet attract?

● What are they made of?

● Are they made of the same material?

● Are all objects made of this material magnetic? (Which might need further testing?)

If the children look back at their predictions, they will ascertain whether they were 'right' or not.

● Were you surprised?

● Have you changed your mind now that you've done the test?

Magnetism

There are three magnetic metals: iron, nickel and cobalt. Iron is the most widely used of these metals, commonly in the form of steel. Steel is over 95% iron with traces of carbon, and sometimes other metals added in alloy steels. For example, stainless steel has chromium and nickel added to prevent it rusting. Some steel contains a high proportion of chromium and is not magnetic.

Magnets themselves are pieces of steel/iron that have been magnetised so that groups of iron atoms (called domains) line up in one particular direction. In an un-magnetised piece of iron the domains are arranged randomly so their magnetic effect is cancelled out.

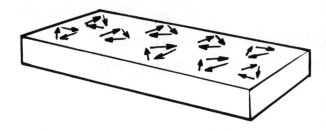

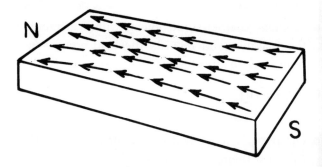

A range of magnets is available to buy from suppliers, including powerful alnico alloy magnets. Children should be warned that all magnets will lose their magnetism if knocked about.

Name .... Date ....

Magnetic or not?

Which things do you think are magnetic?

Draw a circle around them.

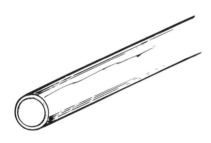

copper pipe

sheet of paper

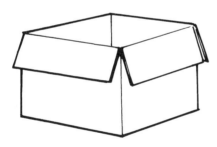

cardboard box

wooden play block

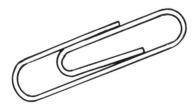

steel paper clip

plastic toy

Name .... Date ....

Magnetic or not?

Which things do you think are magnetic?

We will test these things	I think it will stick to the magnet (yes or no)
copper pipe	
sheet of paper	
cardboard box	
wooden play block	
steel paper clip	
plastic toy	

Name .... Date ....

Magnetic or not?

My results

Things we tested	Does it stick to the magnet? (yes or no)
copper pipe	
sheet of paper	
cardboard box	
wooden play block	
steel paper clip	
plastic toy	

Name .... Date ....

Magnetic or not?

Here are the things we chose to test:

My results

Things we tested	Does it stick to the magnet? (yes or no)

Name .... Date ....

Magnetic or not?

Sort the things you tested into 2 groups.

These things are magnetic	These things are not magnetic

Name .... Date ....

Magnetic or not?

My predictions, results and conclusion

We will test these things	I think it will stick to the magnet (yes or no)	Did it stick to the magnet? (yes or no)

My predictions were right for ....

....

I found out that things made of .... are magnetic.

Name .... Date ....

Magnetic or not?

My recording skills

❑ With help, I can fill in a chart showing which things I think will stick to a magnet.

❑ I can fill in a chart showing which things I think will stick to a magnet.
(Level 1)

❑ I can draw a picture showing which things stick to a magnet.
(Level 1)

❑ I can fill in a simple table showing my predictions and results.
(Level 2)

Sorting and using materials: Testing paper

Nelson Thornes Ref: PS Kit 1.3.3

Learning objectives

Children should learn:

● that materials can be used in a variety of ways

● to **group materials** together and **make a record of groupings**

● to **suggest how to test an idea** about whether a paper is suitable for a particular purpose.

Lesson notes

 Approximate timing: 2 hours

 Warn children about paper cuts to the skin.

Type of enquiry

The first part of this Sc1 enquiry will give children the opportunity to classify different types of paper. Then they test the strength of the papers (recognising the need for fair testing).

Introduction

Introduce the activity by showing the children different types of paper. Ask the class:

● What do we use these types of paper for?

● How are the papers different?

Group work

Ask the groups to think of words that describe the different types of paper.

They sort the papers into different types. Then they can look at the sets chosen by another group and guess how they arrived at their groupings. Record their own types by sticking samples of each paper onto a poster or A3 sheet to display to the rest of the class. Sheets 1, 2 and 3 are suitable (enlarged when photocopied).

Next, introduce the challenge of finding the best paper to wrap a parcel with.

● What does a good paper for wrapping parcels have to be like?

Amongst the suggestions, the strength of the paper can be chosen as the one to test.

● How can we test which paper is strongest?

Let groups discuss the problem and check their ideas with you before trying them out.

Ask groups to record their findings. (See Sheet 4.)

Whole class

At this age most tests suggested will be subjective to some extent; for example, trying to tear or cut each paper and judging which was most difficult to do. Challenge children as to the 'fairness' of these tests (introducing evaluation skills).

● Can you be sure that each test was exactly the same?
● How could you make it a fair test?

At this point you can show strips of paper with a hole punched near one end from which you can hang slotted masses. Test a couple of pieces of paper by adding on masses until the paper tears. Stress the elements of fair testing (same size of paper, hole in same place).

Differentiated Sc1 learning outcomes

Planning

● with help, can suggest ways of testing paper
● suggests how to test the strength of different papers
● with help, recognises the need for fair testing.

Observing

● observes each test as a separate event
● compares differences and similarities between papers as they group them.

Recording

● with help, can make a chart showing types of paper
● constructs own chart showing types of paper
● with help, can fill in tables provided
● fills in tables provided.

Concluding

● with help, sorts papers into groups when given the criteria
● sorts papers into groups consistent with their own criteria
● sequences papers in order of strength from the results of their tests.

Using the differentiated sheets

Sheet 1★ is aimed at children getting used to filling in charts, in this case by sticking samples of paper on the correct part of the sheet. (Level 1)

Sheets 2★★ and 3★★ use two-column tables to help children classify papers and record their results. Sheet 3 is the more challenging as children make their own choice of headings for the table. (The use of a simple table is a Level 2 skill.)

Sheet 4★★ helps children record the sequencing of papers in order of strength. (The basic comparison of observations and sorting them into a sequence is a Level 2 skill.)

Sheet 5★★★ is a skill sheet to help children recognise the need for fair testing.

Sheet 6 is the pupil record sheet to complete for this enquiry. The children will need help filling these in.

Sheets 1 to 4 are best enlarged to A3 size when photocopied.

Background information

Grouping materials

Through observation and comparison, children can sort a collection of things into groups of their own choosing. They make their own decisions about the groups they use. Decision making is a vital part of scientific enquiry. Sorting, or classifying, brings order to their enquiries and in learning about sorting and grouping, they are beginning to learn what classification is all about. This activity gives a very good opportunity for children to make their own decisions and to describe, record and justify them, and to ask others in the class about their ideas.

Recording

After using sorting circles, the children should make a more permanent record for display and to remind them later of what they did. This will also develop descriptive langauge such as rough/smooth, thick/thin, hard/soft.

The children are at an early stage in their understanding of how to use tables to record findings. Enquiries such as this one offer excellent opportunities to model the use of a table and teach children how to read a table. The two-column table with headings provided is the starting point for developing the skill of designing tables; others may choose their own headings for the table when grouping different types of paper.

Suggesting how to test an idea

Given a number of different papers to choose from, the children will come up with a variety of suggestions about which is 'best' for wrapping a parcel: 'It's the prettiest/nicest, it folds easily, you can't see the present through it, it's the strongest', etc....

The first of these suggestions is not suitable for a scientific test (although a survey of the children's opinions could be carried out). The others lend themselves more easily to a practical test.

Ask: How could you test if it folds easily/is not transparent/is the strongest? Give them opportunities to try out their ideas and find out the answers.

During their group work and in the concluding stage of the testing, children can be challenged as to the fairness of the tests they conduct. The skill sheet (Sheet 5) on evaluating the testing of paper is best done after the children have had 'hands-on' experience of trying out their own suggestions.

Strength of paper

The strength of paper is determined by factors such as:

● thickness of paper
● alignment of fibres
● dimensions of fibres
● compression during manufacture
● additives, e.g. fillers.

Looking at the papers provided under magnifying glasses (or perhaps a binocular microscope) will reveal the fibrous structure of the wood pulp fibres.

Name .... Date ....

Sorting out paper

Stick bits of paper in these boxes:

These bits of paper are ....

These bits of paper are ....

Name .... Date ....

Sorting out paper

Stick bits of paper into this table:

These papers are strong	These papers are weak

Name .... Date ....

Sorting out paper

Stick bits of paper into this table:

These papers	These papers ....

Name .... Date ....

Which paper is strongest?

Put the papers you tested into order:

Type of paper	Order of strength (1, 2, 3, 4 or 5)

Name .... Date ....

Which paper is strongest?

A group tested 4 different papers to see which was strongest.

Look at their test below:

Talk about:

Is this a fair test?

Explain your ideas to your partner.

How could you make this a fair test?

Name .... Date ....

Which paper is strongest?

My planning skills

❑ With help, I can suggest how to test the strength of paper.
(Level 1/2)

❑ I can suggest how to test the strength of paper.
(Level 2)

❑ With help, I can see when a test is not fair.
(Level 2)

❑ I can see for myself when a test is not really fair.
(Level 2/3)

My recording skills

❑ With help, I can make a chart showing different types of paper.

❑ I can make a chart showing different types of paper.
(Level 1)

❑ I can fill in a simple results table for different types of paper.
(Level 2)

❑ I can put different types of paper in order of strength in my results table.
(Level 2)

Sorting and using materials: Is it waterproof?

Learning objectives

Children should learn:

- to **suggest how to test** whether materials are waterproof
- to **explore ways of answering the question**
- to **communicate what they did and what happened, making simple comparisons**
- to use what happened to **draw a conclusion** and to **say what they found out.**

Lesson notes

 Approximate timing: 1.5 hours

Type of enquiry

This Sc1 enquiry will give children the opportunity to explore materials and test their suitability as a waterproof barrier (recognising the need for fair testing).

Introduction

Introduce the activity by showing the children a doll's house. It has a leaking roof and needs to be repaired. Ask the class:

- Why do we need a roof on houses?
- Which materials do we use to make roofs?
- What could we use to mend the roof of the doll's house?
- What other things need to be waterproof?

Show children the fabrics and materials you are going to test to see which are waterproof/won't let water through.

Group work

Groups are given samples of materials to test and discuss how to test which ones are waterproof. Stress that we want to find materials that do not let water through. Gather ideas from groups. Show how you can fasten a piece of material across the top of a plastic container using an elastic band. Make a hollow in the material to pour the water into. Children with sensible alternative methods can use their own ideas.

Challenge fairness of test by suggesting that it doesn't matter if they pour lots of water on one material but a small amount on another. Some will recognise the need to use the same amount of water.

● Why will it be best to use small amounts of water?

Time is another factor that should be considered.

Groups conduct their tests and record what happens. (Use sheet 1, 2 or 3) It is best to give each group the same number of containers as materials to test. This makes comparison of materials easier.

Whole class

Get feedback on how testing went and on the results. Some materials will let no water through. These are waterproof. Of the others, some will let more water through than others.

● Which material was best?
● Can we put them in order? (Sheet 4)

Reinforce concept of fair testing:

● How did we make it a fair test? (Sheet 5)

Differentiated Sc1 learning outcomes

Planning

● with help, can suggest ways of testing which materials are waterproof
● suggests how to test which materials are waterproof
● with help, recognises the need for fair testing in a simple context
● recognises the need for fair testing in a simple context.

Observing

● observes each test as a separate event
● compares differences between amounts of water let through.

Recording

● with help, can make a chart showing groups of waterproof/not waterproof materials
● constructs own chart showing groups of waterproof/not waterproof materials
● with help, can fill in tables provided
● fills in tables provided.

Concluding

● with help, sorts materials into groups when given the criteria
● sorts materials into groups consistent with their own criteria
● sequences materials in order of ability to stop water getting through from the results of their tests.

Using the differentiated sheets

Sheet 1★ is aimed at children getting used to filling in charts, in this case by sticking samples of material on the correct side of the sheet. Encourage children to label their materials. (Level 1)

Sheets 2★★ and 3★★ use two- and three-column tables to help children classify materials and record their results. Samples of materials can be stuck on the tables or words can be used. (The use of a simple table is a Level 2 skill.)

Sheet 4★★ helps children record the sequencing of materials in order of their ability to resist water getting through. (The basic comparison of observations to produce a sequence is a Level 2 skill.)

Sheet 5★★★ is a skill sheet to help children recognise the need for fair testing.

Sheet 6★★★ prompts children to record how they made their tests fair.

Sheet 7 is the pupil record sheet to complete for this enquiry. The children will need help filling these in or the teacher might prefer to complete the sheet themselves.

Background information

Planning

The children will come up with suggestions to test if a fabric is waterproof such as 'put them out in the rain' or 'put them in water'. It's important here to develop the notion of an identical 'test' for each fabric and that indoors is best for this one. Take a feasible idea from the children or use the one suggested earlier. Then ask how we will know which material is waterproof.

This develops the ideas of evidence gathering — using evidence from observation and, perhaps in this case, measurement.

The teacher can then introduce elements of fair testing. The technique of modelling the blatantly 'unfair test' can stimulate responses that allow children to make decisions for themselves in these early stages of planning fair tests.

Communicating and making simple comparisons

As communication is such an important part of the learning process, allow time and encourage the children to talk about what happens in their tests with each other and to you. Examples of useful language to use when describing and comparing are: more than/less than, none/some/a lot/all, quickly/slowly, slower/faster. Putting their results into a table will help them develop a clear idea of what they observed.

Waterproof materials

Sheets of plastic have no fibres for water to pass between. They are made of very long molecules called polymers. Materials, such as cotton or silk, are also made of polymers but during manufacture these are spun into fibres which are then woven together to make fabrics. The density of the weave is an important factor in a fabric's resistance to penetration by water. The absorbency of the fabric as it soaks up water also affects the results of this enquiry, so that an absorbent material can be judged to be waterproof if you go solely on the volume of water that passes through. It is better to look at the water left on top of the material as well, to judge how waterproof, as opposed to absorbent, a material is. A good example of this is wool, which resists the water which rests on the fabric for a long time, then it is absorbed and some goes through the fabric.

Name .... Date ....

Is it waterproof?

Stick bits of material in these boxes.

Write the names of the materials next to each one.

These bits of material are waterproof.
They don't let water through.

These bits of material are not waterproof.
They let water through.

Name .... Date ....

Is it waterproof?

Stick bits of material and write their names in this table:

These materials are waterproof.	These materials are not waterproof.

Name .... Date ....

Is it waterproof?

Stick bits of material and write their names in this table:

These are waterproof. They let no water through.	These materials let a bit of water through.	These materials let lots of water through.

Name .... Date ....

Is it waterproof?

Put the materials you tested into order:

Type of material	Order of dryness underneath (1, 2, 3, 4 or 5, where 1 is best at keeping water out)

Name .... Date ....

Is it waterproof?

We tested our materials like this:

How did you make this a fair test?
Write down 2 things you did:

1. ....

....

2. ....

....

Name .... Date ....

Is it waterproof?

A group tested four different materials to see which was most waterproof.

Look at their test below:

Talk about:

Is this a fair test?

Explain your ideas to your partner.

How could you make this a fair test?

Name .... Date ....

Is it waterproof?

My planning skills

☐ With help, I can suggest how to test which materials are waterproof. (Level 1/2)

☐ I can suggest how to test which materials are waterproof. (Level 2)

☐ With help, I can see when a test is not fair. (Level 2)

☐ I can see for myself when a test is not really fair. (Level 2/3)

My recording skills

☐ With help, I can make a chart showing which materials are waterproof and which are not.

☐ I can make a chart showing which materials are waterproof and which are not. (Level 1)

☐ I can fill in a simple table showing which materials are waterproof and which are not. (Level 2)

☐ I can put different materials in order of how well they keep water out. Then I can show the order in my results table. (Level 2)

Sound and hearing:
How far away can we hear sounds?

Nelson Thornes Ref: PS Kit 1.6.5

Learning objectives

Children should learn:

- that sounds get fainter as they travel away from a source
- to **measure distances** using non-standard (or standard) measures
- to **make and record their measurements.**

Lesson notes

 Approximate timing: 2 hours

Type of enquiry

This Sc1 enquiry will give the children the opportunity to explore and measure how far sounds travel.

Introduction

Introduce the activity by asking the children about loud and quiet sounds. Ask for examples of each. Ask if a loud sound (such as that from an aeroplane engine) is always loud. When is it loudest? Does it matter how far away the aeroplane is from you? Explore how sounds get louder or fainter as the sound moves towards or away from us.

In the hall or playground:

Group the children with their backs to you, ask them to raise their hands when they can hear a sound. Make a loud sound, then a quiet sound.

Move a source of quiet sound from where it is inaudible to them, to where the majority can hear it. Measure how far away they can hear it.

Ask the children to suggest ideas for measuring distance.

Some ideas using non-standard measures in various ways are:

- pace out the distance, or use the floor tiles, for counting in non-standard units
- use a long piece of cord or rope for making comparisons: more than, less than
- the children join hands at arms' length to measure longer distances in non-standard units.

Repeat, this time using a sound source close to the children, e.g. a small bell (outdoors) or a ticking clock (indoors), and measure how far away it is when they can no longer hear it. Other sounds could be — children talking, music playing, shakers, footsteps.

Try moving to the sides of the hall or playground.

Individual and group work

As appropriate the children use standard or non-standard measures. They can use a metre stick, trundle wheel or tape to measure in standard units.

Ensure that each child does some measuring and records their work. (Sheets 1 to 5)

Ask the children what they found out:

● What did we do first?
● Could we hear the loud sound?
● Could we hear the quiet sound?
● When the source of the sound got nearer/ further away, how did it change?
● So what is the pattern?

Whole class

Ask individuals or groups of children to explain how they measured how far they could hear sounds. Ask for examples of how many units of distance they could/could not hear things. (Work on recording and drawing conclusions from these results continues later in the QCA Scheme.)

Using the differentiated sheets

Sheet 1★ Skills practice. This is a group activity with help from the teacher. The children can practise measuring distance by counting paces. Make a large version of the table for class recording; the questions may be answered orally or recorded by the teacher or the children. (Using a simple chart is a Level 1 activity.)

Sheet 2★ The children use the box to draw the activity to show the distance from the teacher to themselves. (Using a simple chart is a Level 1 activity.)

Sheet 3★★ In groups or pairs, the children measure and record the source of sounds and the distance in non-standard measures (paces). They make a simple analysis of their findings. (Level 2/3)

Sheet 4★★ Here, the children use a different non-standard measure and begin to consider accuracy of measurement. They make a simple analysis of their results. (Using simple tables — Level 2.)

Sheet 5★★★ Using standard measures, the children record and analyse their measurements. (Using simple equipment to measure is a Level 3 activity.)

Sheet 6 Differentiated outcomes for children at Levels 2 and 3.

Differentiated Sc1 learning outcomes

Measuring distances/length

● watches the teacher or other children, measures and records results with help
● knows the terms — near, far, length, distance
● measures independently
● measures in non-standard units, counting to 20
● measures in non-standard units, counting to 100
● uses metre sticks, trundle wheels, tape measures to measure distance/length.

Making and recording their measurements

● counts to 20 and writes the number in a table
● counts to 100 and uses a table to record the distance/length
● records several measurements using non-standard units in a table
● records several measurements using standard units in a table.

Background information

Measuring length/distance

At this age, many of the children are developing the concepts of 'distance', 'length', 'near', 'far', 'more than', 'less than'. Once they understand the meaning of these terms, they can use measurement to give them some useful information. In this investigation, they are exploring the nature of sound and how it travels. To find out how far it travels requires measurement. Measurement techniques are much better taught when they are needed, as here. When set in a practical context, the process is much more meaningful.

Sound

Sound is a form of energy and is made when something vibrates. It travels by waves, but there must be some kind of material for the sound to travel through, for example, air, gases, water, solids, for us to hear it. If we were in space we could hear no sounds, even the biggest explosion possible — the Big Bang, for example, would have been inaudible!

Name .... Date ....

How far away can we hear sounds?

Ask a friend to use a shaker to make a sound, then walk away slowly.

Stop when you can't hear it any more. Mark the spot. Then count how many paces it takes to get back to the shaker.

Write down the distance on the chart.

Try again with something which makes a louder/quieter sound, like a small bell, or a friend's voice. Write the distance on the chart.

Object	Paces

Which takes the highest number of paces?

Which is the longest distance?

Which sound travels the furthest?

Which takes the least paces?

Which is the shortest length?

Which sound travels the shortest distance?

Name .... Date ....

How far away can we hear sounds?

Make a drawing of the children listening and how far away your teacher was when you could no longer hear the

....

Name .... Date ....

How far away can we hear sounds?

We measured how far away we could hear loud and quiet sounds.

Record your measurements in this table:

Sound source	We could hear it as far as this

Which sound came from the furthest away?

Was this the loudest sound?

How far could you hear the quietest sound?

Name .... Date ....

How far away can we hear sounds?

We measured how far sound travels with a line of children like this:

We stretched our arms out straight.

Here are our results:

Source of sound	How far we could hear it

Which was the loudest sound? ....

Which sound travelled the shortest distance? ....

Which was the quietest sound? ....

Name .... Date ....

How far away can we hear sounds?

Record your measurements in this table:

Sound source	How far we could hear it (m or cm)

Think about these questions with your teacher:

Which sound travelled from furthest away?

Was this the loudest sound?

How far did the quietest sound travel?

What happens to sound as it travels away from you?

What happens to sound as it travels towards you?

Name .... Date ....

How far away can we hear sounds?

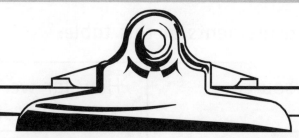

Measuring distances

❑ I can measure length and distance using ....
(non-standard measures — Level 2)

❑ I can measure length and distance in ....

❑ I used a .... to measure.
(standard measures — Level 3)

Recording measurements

❑ I can make and record my measurements in a
simple table.
(Level 2)

Plants and animals: Finding plants and animals

Nelson Thornes Ref: PS Kit 2.2.1

Learning objectives

Children should learn:

- that there are different kinds of plants and animals in the immediate environment
- to treat animals and the environment with care and sensitivity
- to **recognise hazards** in working with soil
- to **observe and make a record** of animals and plants found
- to **present results in a table**
- to **research simple texts to find information**.

Lesson notes

 Approximate timing: 2 hours

Type of enquiry

This Sc1 enquiry will give the children the opportunity to observe and record animals and plants in the local environment (exploration), and to look in books for simple information about other plants and animals (research and classification).

Arrange to walk through a local area such as the school garden or a park.

Introduction

Introduce the activity by finding out what the children know about plants and animals and their understanding of 'animal' and 'plant'.

- Where have you seen plants/animals?
- We're going to look for them in the ….
- What animals/plants might we find in the garden/park?
- Whereabouts might we find them?

Individual and group work

The children look in different places in the area for plants and animals: in grass, in bushes, in soil, in the air, in trees. Talk about what they find. Encourage them to use their senses — sight, touch, hearing, smell, as appropriate.

- Feel it; look closely at it under a hand lens or in a bug box; watch it move; is it like anything you know?
- Where did you find it?
- What shape/colour/size is it?
- Do you know what it is?
- How many — legs, wings, spots?
- Is it shiny, furry, smooth, slimy?

Make a brief record of what they found. (Sheet 1)

Back in the classroom ask the children to carefully draw some of the plants and animals they saw and record where they found them. (Sheet 2) The children name the ones they know; some children look up others and write their names in the table. (Sheet 3)

Whole class

Talk about what the children found and where.

- What is this?
- Where did you find it?
- Tell us about it — what colour/shape/size is it?
- Is it a plant or an animal?
- What sort of plant or animal is it?
- How do you know?
- Where did you find your information?
- What else could we find out about it?
- What would you like to know?
- Any questions about the animals and plants?

Use the correct vocabulary for where it was found — in, under, behind… .

Stress the observational skills of seeing details — making use of several senses and noticing relevant details of plants and animals and their surroundings.

Differentiated Sc1 learning outcomes

Observing

- finds a living thing — a plant or an animal — and can say where they found it
- describes its shape/colour
- describes, using simple vocabulary, how many — legs/antennae/wings/spots/petals/leaves
- describes what it does/how it moves/where it goes.

Using a table to record results

- describes their observations using simple vocabulary
- uses a simple table to make recordings.

Researching to find simple information

- with help, matches illustrations with what they observed earlier
- with help, uses simple texts to find information
- individually locates relevant books, and uses index
- says how they decided which relevant features helped them name a plant or animal.

Using the differentiated sheets

Sheet 1★/★★ The Field Notebook can be used by the children, with help or independently, to make a brief drawing or record of what they find in the park or garden. (Level 1/2)

Sheet 2★★ asks the children to use boxes to draw an animal or plant and to add some simple writing. (Level 2)

Sheet 3★★ asks the children to observe illustrations of animals, record their observations and to look in books to name them. (To find information in simple texts, with help, is a Level 2 activity.)

Sheet 4★★ is a teacher-led activity to enhance the children's observational skills. (Levels 1 and 2)

Sheet 5★★ asks the children to identify British animals and plants from secondary sources. (Level 2)

Sheet 6 is the record for the children to complete. They will need help at this stage to fill these in.

Background information

Observation

Observing does not simply mean looking and recording. It means using all the senses as appropriate (and safe). It means being alert to the many features that may be observable and not only those that are most obvious. The purpose of developing children's skills of observation is so that they will be able to use all their senses to gather information for their explorations of things around them. Gradually, children can be taught to distinguish the relevant from the irrelevant in the context of a particular investigation or problem.

Encourage the children to make as many observations as they can, giving attention to detail and larger features. The children will be interested and intrigued by the variety of wildlife around them as they explore the park or garden and will be able to notice tiny details and differences between the animals and plants. You can encourage further, larger and deeper observations through discussion, asking questions and encouraging the children to ask questions.

Using a table to record findings

Presenting information in simple, two-column tables helps children to see what they have found out and what is relevant in their observations, for example the features of an exploration that the teacher is focusing on. Here, they are asked to use two-column tables and a table of four boxes in which to put drawings and writing.

Animals and plants

Plants are living organisms which make their own food by the process of photosynthesis. (See also 1B — Growing plants.) Animals, on the other hand, rely on organic matter, that is other animals or plants, for their food.

It is easy to tell that a fox is an animal and a daisy is a plant, but the distinction becomes blurred, for children especially, when it comes to the so-called lower forms of life such as worms and insects. Many children do not think of humans as animals or trees as plants.

All forms of life have common features such as growing, feeding, reproducing, excreting and dying. All have sensitivity and respond to outside factors, so all living things should be treated with care.

Name .... Date ....

Where do plants and animals live?

'Field Notebook'

On the line in the box, write where each plant or animal was found.

What I found and where.

<table>
<tr><td>

....
</td><td>

....
</td></tr>
<tr><td>

....
</td><td>

....
</td></tr>
<tr><td>

....
</td><td>

....
</td></tr>
</table>

Name .... Date ....

Local plants and animals

Draw animals or plants you found.
Write where you found them. Name them if you can.
Choose words to describe each one.

	Where did you find it?
	Describe it here.
	Where did you find it?
	Describe it here.
	Where did you find it?
	Describe it here.

Name .... Date ....

Finding plants and animals

What do you notice about these animals?

What colour, shape, size, how many legs, what else?

What are their names? If you don't know, look in books to find out.

What shape is it?

....

How many legs has it?

....

What else do you see?

....

What is it?

....

What shape is it?

....

How many legs has it?

....

What else do you see?

....

What is it?

....

Name .... Date ....

Finding plants and animals

What is this animal?
Have you ever seen any of these?
Where?
What do you notice about them?
What colours are they?
How big are they?
Where do they live?
What can they do?
How do they move?
What other animal is it like? How is it different from it;
how is it the same?
What does it eat?
Does it have babies?
What other questions can you think of?

Name .... Date ....

Find the names of animals and plants

Use books to find the names of these living things:

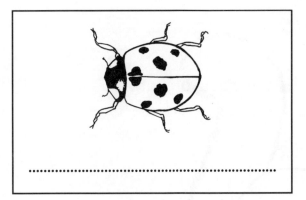

....

....

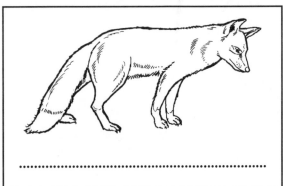

....

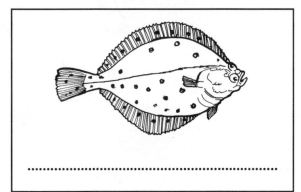

....

....

....

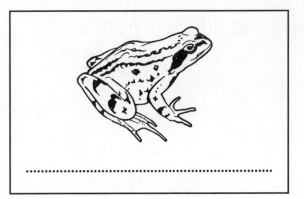

....

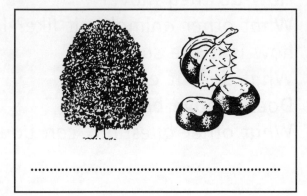

....

Name .... Date ....

Plants and animals

My observing skills

❑ I can find animals and plants in a garden or park. (Level 1)

❑ I can say where I found them. (Level 1)

❑ I can describe their shape and colour and some other details. (Level 1)

❑ I can use a hand lens to look at small animals and plants. (Level 2)

❑ I can use a binocular microscope to see things. (Level 2)

❑ I can describe animals and plants in some detail. (Level 2)

❑ I can describe how an animal moves and where it lives. (Level 2)

❑ I can compare plants and animals. (Level 2)

My recording skills

❑ I can write and draw what I saw in the garden/park in a table. (Level 2)

My research skills

❑ I can match pictures of animals and plants and name them. (Level 1/2)

❑ With help, I can find pictures in books to help me name animals and plants. (Level 2)

❑ I can explain how I decided what the animals and plants are. (Level 3)

Plants and animals:
What do seeds need to germinate?

Nelson Thornes Ref: PS Kit 2.2.4

Learning objectives

Children should learn:

- to **turn ideas of their own**, about what plants need to begin to grow, **into a form that can be tested**
- to **observe and make a day-by-day record of observations**
- to **use the results to draw a conclusion** about what seeds need to begin to grow and **decide whether this is what they expected**
- that seeds produce new plants.

Lesson notes

 Approximate timing: 2 hours plus time to record results at intervals over 10 days

Type of enquiry

This Sc1 activity will give the children the opportunity to complete a biological enquiry (with elements of fair testing) to find out the conditions needed for germination.

Introduction

Introduce the activity by showing the children a handful of various seeds — peas, beans, grass, sunflowers.

- What are these? What do they do?
- Remember from Year 1 — do plants need light to grow well?
- But what do you think seeds need to help them begin to grow?

Talk about the suggestions, choose practical examples — water, soil/compost.

- Can we turn these into questions?
- Do seeds need water to begin to grow?
- Do seeds need compost to start to grow?
- Who thinks seeds do need water/do not need water? Who isn't sure?
- So how could we do an investigation to find out?
- What might you see if they begin to grow?

Divide the class into two groups, the 'water' groups and the 'compost' groups.

Plan the activity together — water groups: seeds with water: others without — compost groups, seeds on compost, sand, kitchen paper. Keep all other conditions the same. Cover all the trays of seeds with cling film to stop them drying out too soon.

Individual and group work

Help groups to set up their investigations. (Use several seeds in case some do not germinate.)

Help them to record their results at regular intervals, over about 10 days. (Sheets 1, 2 and 3)

Discuss the results with each group.

Whole class

Talk about all the results — any differences? Did any seeds not germinate?

Discuss how well they did their test and any problems that occurred.

Come to a conclusion:

- Do seeds need water to germinate?
- Do seeds need compost to germinate?
- Was this what you expected?

Use Sheets 4 and 5 to reinforce the conclusions and assess their predictions.

Differentiated Sc1 learning outcomes

Turning their own ideas into a form that can be tested

- suggests ideas, some of which are testable — they need water; others not — they need TLC
- turns a testable idea into a question — Do seeds need water to begin to grow?

Observing and making a day-to-day record of observations

- looks for changes in the seeds, roots and shoots from one day to the next
- makes comparisons from one day to the next
- records the changes at intervals during the 10 days with drawings in a simple table
- records the changes using scientific vocabulary in a table.

Using the results to draw a conclusion

- puts the information from the results together and deduces something from this
- from the results deduces that seeds do need water to germinate, but they do not need compost.

Deciding whether this is what they expected

- says what they predicted
- checks their prediction against their results
- increases their understanding in the light of evidence.

Using the differentiated sheets

Sheet 1★★ gives the children practice in thinking how to collect data to answer a question. (Level 2)

Sheet 2★ asks the children to make a day-to-day record of observations and to answer the original question. (Level 1)

Sheet 3★★ asks for the children to record day-to-day observations in a table and describe what happens. (Level 2)

Sheet 4★★ may follow Sheet 2 and asks the children to consider their results, come to a conclusion and check their prediction against their findings. (Level 2)

Sheet 5★★ asks about the need for soil/compost in germination. (Level 2/3)

Sheet 6 is the children's own record of their achievements in this activity.

Background information

Turning ideas into a form that can be tested

Framing a question, based on a prediction, will turn the prediction into a form that can be tested.

'I think seeds need soil to begin to grow',
becomes
'Do seeds need soil to germinate?'

Most investigations are based on a question, but one of a certain kind. Science-related questions are about what there is in the world and how it behaves.

Where children are encouraged, they will come up with many questions, but these aren't all testable. For example, we cannot test scientifically a question such as Which seeds are the most attractive? But we can test Which seeds will germinate the fastest?

Observing day-to-day changes

This is a good opportunity for children to develop their skills of observing similarities, differences, changes over time and links between one feature and another.

Making a day-to-day record of observations

Recording the changes in seeds over time will fix the changes in the child's mind before they are forgotten. If the children draw the seeds as they germinate, they will be able to see the process of germination as it takes place. The process of recording underlines the teaching and gives the children a real and personal experience. At this stage, many will be able to describe what is happening orally or in writing and some will be able to assimilate the more scientific language, such as the parts of the plant, as they emerge.

Drawing a conclusion

Two aspects of concluding are developed in this activity — drawing a conclusion from the results and checking a prediction.

During the 10 days of observation, you can begin to answer the question being investigated:

● Have any of the seeds germinated?
● Which ones?
● Does it look as if they might need water/not need compost?

When the results are all recorded, individuals and groups of children can be asked about their conclusions before the whole class draws a conclusion from the evidence.

Other conclusions can be drawn from the evidence, such as 'Not all seeds germinate'. But as this does not answer the question, treat it as something extra that the children have found out and perhaps take the opportunity to talk about the importance of sample size in this type of inquiry and other things they noticed.

Matching a prediction to the conclusion

Young children will often use the word 'guess' to describe what they think will happen. Sometimes, these guesses are based on their experiences. Ask them 'Why do you think that?' If there is a reason which is consistent with their 'guess', tell them this is, in fact, what we call a prediction, not a guess, to help them make the distinction for themselves.

At this stage, as well as remembering their prediction and not changing it, the children should now be able to decide whether the conclusion is what was expected. Recording predictions helps in this process. Also, they will begin to develop their knowledge in the light of evidence that may be contrary to what they originally thought.

Seeds and germination

All seeds contain an embryo with the potential to grow into a mature plant similar to other members of its species. Most seeds also contain food reserves which are used during the early stages of germination. When a seed absorbs water it swells, then, after a few days, the root emerges and absorbs more water from the soil, and finally, the shoot emerges. This is the process of germination.

Name .... Date ....

What do you think seeds need to make them start to grow?

Make a list in this table. Then think how you could make a test to find out. One has been done and another one has been started for you.

What seeds need to start to grow	How we could test to find out
Water	Set two pots of seeds, give one some water and one no water.
Soil (or compost)	

Name .... Date ....

Do seeds need water to begin to grow?

I think that seeds ....

I drew the seeds to show what happened:

	With water	Without water
After .... days		
After .... days		
After .... days		
After .... days		
After .... days		

Name .... Date ....

Do seeds need water to begin to grow?

My prediction ....

My results

	With water	Without water
After .... days		
What happened		
After .... days		
What happened		
After .... days		
What happened		
After .... days		
What happened		
After .... days		
What happened		

Name .... Date ....

Do seeds need water to begin to grow?

Looking at our results

Which seeds began to grow?

....

Did all the seeds with water begin to grow?

....

Did any of the seeds without water begin to grow?

....

Do seeds need water to begin to grow?

....

What did you predict?

....

What do you think now?

....

Draw one of the seeds that has grown the most and name the roots and the shoot.

Name .... Date ....

Do seeds need soil/compost to germinate?

My prediction ....

What we did. ....

....

....

What happened

After .... days ....

After .... days ....

After .... days ....

After .... days ....

After .... days ....

Our results

The seeds germinated in ....

The seeds did not germinate in ....

Our conclusion is that ....

....

My prediction was that ....

....

The result ....what I expected

Do seeds need soil/compost to germinate? ....

Name .... Date ....

What do seeds need to germinate?

My questioning skills

☐ I can suggest an idea to test. (Level 1/2)

☐ I can turn an idea into a question that we can test. (Level 2)

My observing skills

☐ I can see the changes in the seeds that begin to grow. (Level 1)

☐ I can compare the changes over time. (Level 2)

My recording skills

☐ I can record day-to-day changes with drawings. (Level 1)

☐ I can record day-to-day changes in a table. (Level 2)

☐ I can describe the changes, using the names for parts of the plant. (Level 2)

My concluding skills

☐ I can use these results to answer our question. (Level 2)

☐ I can say whether what happened was what I expected. (Level 2)

Variation: Hand spans, foot size and length of arm

Nelson Thornes Ref: PS Kit 2.3.5

Learning objectives

Children should learn:

- that some differences between themselves and other children can be measured
- to **measure hand span in standard units of length** (to the nearest centimetre)
- to **present measurements in block graphs**
- to **make comparisons** of hand span
- to **raise questions** about differences between themselves, **test them and decide whether their predictions were correct.**

Lesson notes

 Approximate timing: 2 hours

Type of enquiry

This Sc1 enquiry will give children the opportunity to explore differences between themselves and their classmates and to look for patterns in data they collect. This is an enquiry set in a biological context.

Introduction

Show children how to measure hand span from the tip of their thumb to the tip of their little finger. Explain that we are going to collect the measurements for the whole class and show the results on a block graph.

Group work

Children measure their hand span and report it to the teacher who completes a group tally chart. Alternatively, children can record their own hand spans and compile their own tally chart. (Sheet 1)

Show the class the layout of the block graph and let children attempt to draw their own graphs on 1 cm square paper. (Sheet 2) Point out the differences between measurements and how the block graph shows this.

Then ask the class if they think that people with the biggest hand spans also have the biggest feet.

Groups measure their feet and record results in a table. (Sheet 3)

Whole class

Choose a dividing line to determine those with big, as opposed to small, hand spans. Do the same with measurements of feet. (Sheet 3) Then plot the results onto a Carroll diagram. (Sheet 4) This can be demonstrated for some groups, but others might be able to attempt the exercise themselves once guidance has been offered.

Comment on the distribution of people plotted to see if there is a link between hand span and foot size. Mention how important the number of people we measure (size of sample) is in this type of enquiry.

Differentiated Sc1 learning outcomes

Predicting

● with help, predicts whether there is a link between hand span and foot size

● predicts whether there is a link between hand span and foot size.

Observing

● with help, measures hand spans to nearest centimetre

● measures hand spans to nearest centimetre.

Recording

● with help, can fill in charts provided

● fills in charts provided

● with help, can fill in tables provided

● fills in tables provided

● with help, can draw a block graph

● can draw a block graph.

Concluding

● with help, checks correctly against predictions

● checks correctly against predictions

● can identify simple patterns.

Using the differentiated sheets

Sheet 1★★ is used to collect data in a tally chart. (Level 2 — simple tables)

Sheet 2★★★ provides the axes for drawing the block graph showing hand spans. (This can be used as evidence for recording 'in a variety of ways' at Level 3.)

Sheet 3★★★ provides a format for recording hand span and foot size, as well as categorising each entry as large or small.

Sheet 4★★★ helps children spot a pattern between hand spans and foot sizes. (Spotting simple patterns is a Level 3 skill.)

Sheet 5★★★ lets children practise the skills of drawing block graphs and can be used in preparation for this lesson.

Sheet 6★★★ gives children the chance to practise spotting a pattern from a Carroll diagram. (Level 3)

Sheet 7 is the pupil record sheet to complete for this enquiry. Some children will need help filling these in.

Background information

Measurement

The children are becoming familiar with centimetres from maths lessons and this activity offers an opportunity to measure in a real-life context. Very often estimations and rough measurements are much more meaningful to young children than precise measurements, so ask them to compare the size of various parts of their hands with those of the other children. Then focus on hand spans, which they now measure to the nearest centimetre. They can compare their estimates with what they found by measuring.

Recording

This enquiry, in the context of Sc2, gives children the chance to record in a variety of ways. There will be opportunities to use tally charts, tables, Carroll diagrams and block graphs. Many children will still need assistance in completing one or more of the methods listed above.

Making comparisons

Once the children have the data on their charts, they can see the range of hand spans, the largest and smallest, the most common hand spans and have a chance to spot patterns in the results. They may also see how much more accurate these results are than their estimates. In subsequent tests, comparing feet and hand sizes, for example, the children may improve their estimates so that their predictions are more firmly based on careful observation.

This enquiry is a good opportunity to teach the importance of sample size and the anomalous ('strange') results that biological data collection can yield. The more people we test, the more certain we can be of any pattern spotted.

Variation

There are two categories of variation in living things: continuous and discontinuous (discrete) variation. Hand span is an example of continuous variation in which we can have any value of length possible within its range. Discontinuous variation can only have specific values, for example, our blood type.

Name .... Date ....

Hand spans

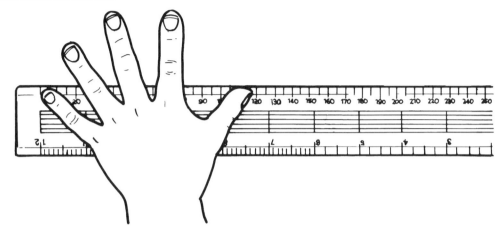

Use the tally chart below to record the hand span of everyone in your class.

Hand span (cm)	Tally (for example, ⅢⅢ I)	Total number

Name .... Date ....

Hand spans

Record the hand spans of your class on a block graph.
(Each block should touch the one next to it.)

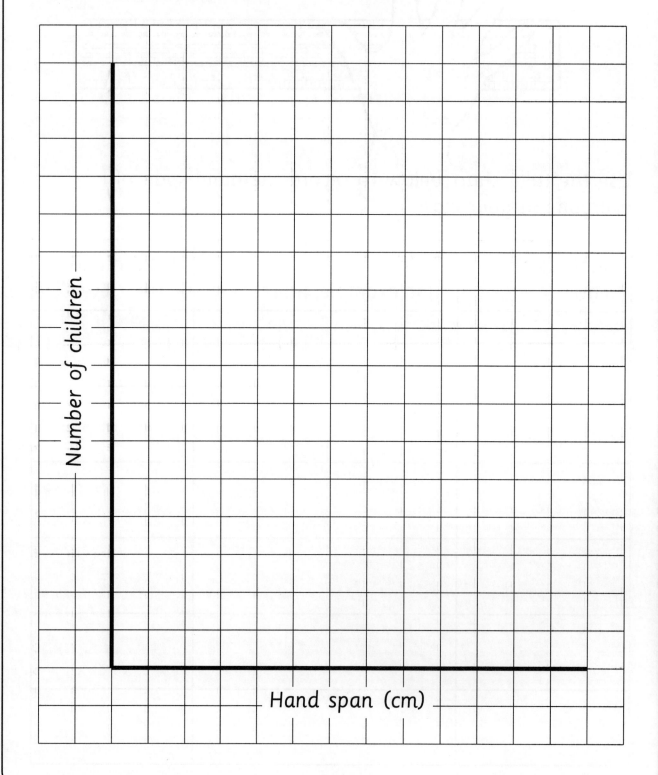

Number of children

Hand span (cm)

Name .... Date ....

Hand span and foot size

Measure your hand span and the length of your foot.
Record your class results in the table below.
Decide if each hand span and foot size is big or small.

Name	Hand span (cm)	Big or small?	Foot size (cm)	Big or small?

Name .... Date ....

Hand span and foot size

Put a cross in one of the boxes for each person in your class.

big

small

small   **big**

foot size

Now answer these questions:

1. Do your results show that:

☐ people with a small hand span always have small feet?

☐ people with a small hand span always have big feet?

☐ people with a small hand span usually have small feet?

☐ people with a small hand span usually have big feet?

☐ there is no pattern?

2. Was your prediction right? ....

Name .... Date ....

Block graph

A group of children measured the length of their arms.
Look at their results in the table below:

Length of arm (cm)	Number of children
36	1
37	3
38	6
39	8
40	7
41	4
42	2

Show their results on a block graph below:

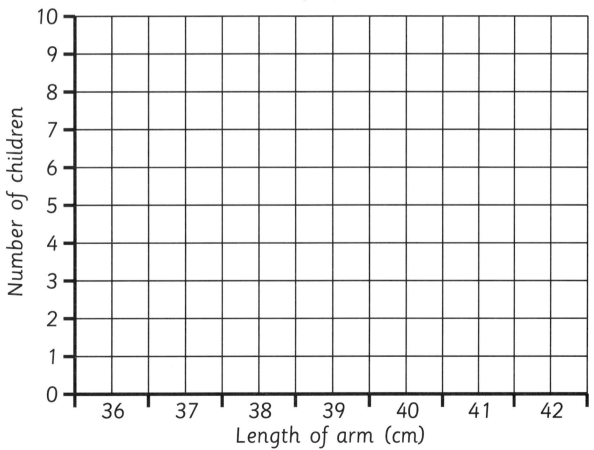

Name .... Date ....

Spot the pattern

A group of children were investigating a question:

Do people with long arms throw a ball further than people with short arms?

Look at their results below:

	short arms	**long arms**
long throw	Jack Alex Hassan	Pat Joe Ali Joanne Sam Carl Ben
short throw	Phil Sue Grace Colin Tracy Liz Nina	Harry Pete Maria

Talk about their results:

Think about the question they asked at the start.

Is it true to say that the longer your arms, the further you can throw a ball?

Name .... Date ....

Hand span, foot size and length of arm

My recording skills

☐ With help, I can make a tally chart.
(Level 1)

☐ I can make a tally chart.
(Level 2)

☐ I can fill in a simple table showing hand spans.
(Level 2)

☐ I can draw a block graph with some help.
(Level 3)

My concluding skills

☐ With help, I can check if my prediction was right.

☐ I can check if my prediction was right.
(Level 2)

☐ I can spot if there is a pattern between hand span
and foot size.
(Level 3)

Grouping and changing materials:
Which is the warmest place?

Nelson Thornes Ref: PS Kit 2.4.5

Learning objectives

Children should learn:

● to use their knowledge about what makes ice melt to **plan what to do**

● to **recognise what would make a test unfair**

● to **use a table to make a record of observations**

● to **use results to draw a conclusion** about which place is warmest.

Lesson notes

 Approximate timing: 2 hours

Type of enquiry

This Sc1 enquiry will give children the opportunity to carry out a fair test, using ice cubes to find out the warmest place in the classroom or school.

Introduction

The children will have had a chance to explore ice melting in a previous lesson. Remind them of this work, then introduce the investigation: 'How can we use our ice cubes to find the warmest place in the classroom or school?'

Ask for suggestions from the class — time how long the ice takes to melt in different places, measure the size of the ice every 15 minutes. Challenge the class by showing them two very differently sized pieces of ice to use in two different places. Their previous explorations with ice should help the children understand the unfairness of this test and reinforce the need to use ice cubes of equal size. (Sheet 6 asks children to evaluate a group's ideas about how to carry out this investigation.)

Group work

Children set up their investigations. Four or five different locations might be chosen (this could be reduced for lower attaining children). The children observe their ice cubes every 15 minutes and record their observations. Measurement of the ice cubes as time passes is difficult, but some higher attaining children may consider this.

A range of sheets for recording observations (and sequencing places) is provided. (Sheets 1, 2, 3 and 4)

Whole class

Help the children focus on the purpose of the investigation by asking:

● Which ice cube melted most quickly?

● Can you put all the ice cubes in order?

● So which place was the warmest?

● Can we check our conclusion in any way?

Also ask about any difficulties/problems the children encountered doing their tests. Ask for suggestions as to how these could be overcome.

Sheet 3 can support children drawing their conclusions.

Differentiated Sc1 learning outcomes

Planning

● with help, can suggest ways of testing which is the warmest place in the room/school

● suggests how to test which is the warmest place in the room/school

● with help, recognises the need for fair testing in simple context

● recognises the need for fair testing in simple context (same sized ice cubes).

Observing

● observes each test as a separate event

● compares ice cubes as they melt

● compares ice cubes as they melt at regular time intervals

● measures ice cubes as they melt at regular time intervals.

Recording

● with help, can fill in charts provided

● fills in charts provided

● with help, can fill in tables provided

● fills in tables provided

● designs own table within which to record results.

Concluding

● with help, can identify the warmest place from their results

● can identify the warmest place from their results

● can sequence the locations in order using their results

● can sequence the locations in order using their results and offer a simple explanation.

Using the differentiated sheets

Sheet 1★ is aimed at those getting used to filling in charts, in this case by drawing ice cubes. A separate chart can be used for each place tested. (This is a Level 1 skill.)

Sheets 2★★, 3★★ and 4★★★ offer different formats of table to record results. Sheet 2 is filled in for each place tested, whereas Sheet 4 is more complex as it combines all results into one table. Sheet 3 supports children in the concluding stage of the investigation, using a table to record the order in which ice cubes melted. (The use of a simple table is a Level 2 skill.)

Sheet 5★★★ helps with planning a fair test. (Level 3)

Sheet 6★★★ focuses children on the need for fair testing. (Level 3)

Sheet 7 is the pupil record sheet to complete for this enquiry. Some children will need help filling these in.

Background information

Planning

This investigation involves the children in using scientific knowledge about ice melting to help them answer a question — Which is the warmest place in the classroom? Through discussion, the children will work out that the ice will melt the fastest in the warmest place. Many of the children will be able to make their own decisions about how to do the test. They will have some ideas about the answer to the question, but they may not be aware that a comparison is needed, and that ice must be put in several different places and not just where they think it is warmest.

Recognising what would make a test unfair

Use the children's suggestions to introduce elements of fair testing to be considered. The technique of the teacher modelling the blatantly 'unfair test', using two obviously different sizes and shapes of ice cube, can stimulate responses that allow children to make decisions to control variables themselves when planning fair tests.

Recording

This investigation requires recording of observations (or measurements) over relatively long periods of time. This presents children with difficulties when comparing successive results and requires careful observations that can be recorded in words, drawings or numbers.

Using results to draw a conclusion

The children will have begun to draw conclusions before the end of their observations, but will still need to look carefully at their results before drawing a conclusion from the activity. The ice cube that melted first will be in the warmest place in the classroom — but what if two ice cubes melted in similar times? What if other groups had different results? Did we do a fair test? Which is the warmest place in the classroom?

Ice melting

As a solid melts and turns into its liquid state you expect its particles to move slightly further apart and the liquid to occupy a slightly larger volume than the solid. However, this is not the case when ice melts. The water particles (H_2O molecules) in ice are held in a lattice that has lots of space between its particles. When this open structure breaks down as the ice melts, the water particles can actually approach each other more closely than in the solid state. Therefore, we get the strange example of a solid that is less dense than its liquid, explaining why ice floats on water!

Name .... Date ....

Which is the warmest place?

I left this ice cube ....

Here is what it looked like:

At the start

After 15 minutes

After 30 minutes

After 45 minutes

After 60 minutes (one hour)

It had all melted after ....
minutes.

Name .... Date ....

Which is the warmest place?

I left this ice cube ....

Time (minutes)	My observations of the ice cube

Name .... Date ....

Which is the warmest place?

My conclusion

Here is the order in which my ice cubes melted:

Place where we left the ice cube	The ice cubes melted in this order (quickest is 1, slowest is 4)

Cross out the wrong word:

The ice cube that melted most quickly was in the warmest/coldest place.

Name .... Date ....

Which is the warmest place?

Time (minutes)	Place where I left my ice cubes			

Name .... Date ....

Which is the warmest place?

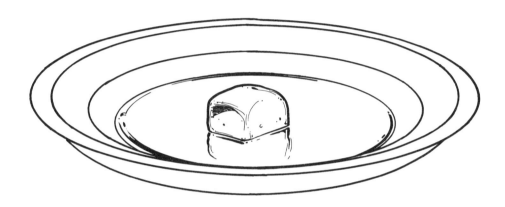

My plan

We will choose .... places to leave our ice cubes.

We will look at them every .... minutes or until they have melted completely.

In our test:

We will change the place that we ....

We will observe/measure ....

We will keep these things the same:

....

....

....

Name .... Date ....

Which is the warmest place?

A group were finding out which place in their classroom was warmest.

Look at the picture below:

Make a list of things the group should do to get better results.

Think about fair testing and safety.

....

....

....

....

....

Name .... Date ....

Which is the warmest place?

My planning skills

☐ With help, I can suggest how to test which place is warmest using ice cubes. (Level 1/2)

☐ I can suggest how to test which place is warmest using ice cubes. (Level 2)

☐ With help, I can see when a test is not fair. (Level 2)

☐ I can see when a test is not really fair and explain why. (Level 3)

My recording skills

☐ With help, I can make a chart showing how ice cubes melt.

☐ I can make a chart showing how ice cubes melt. (Level 1)

☐ I can fill in a simple table showing how ice cubes melt. (Level 2)

☐ I can put places in order of how warm they are in a table. (Level 2)

☐ I can fill in one large table that shows all my results and the order of warmness. (Level 3)

☐ I can design my own results table. (Level 3)

Forces and movement:
Which cars are the best rollers?

Nelson Thornes Ref: PS Kit 2.5.4

Learning objectives

Children should learn:

- to **suggest a question to test and predict what will happen**
- to **decide what to do and what measurements to make**
- to **make measurements and record these in a prepared table**
- to **use results to make comparisons and to evaluate whether the test was fair**
- to **say whether the prediction was correct and to try to explain the results**.

Lesson notes

 Approximate timing: 2 hours

Type of enquiry

This Sc1 enquiry will give the children the opportunity to plan and carry out a whole investigation.

Introduction

Introduce the activity by setting up a variety of ramps and rolling cars down them onto a hard floor. Give each group of children plenty of time to explore what happens for themselves. Ask them to find out what makes a difference to how far a car travels.

Bring them together and ask them about their ideas:

- What made a difference to how the cars rolled down the ramp?
  (Height of the ramp, how much push they give the car, where they start the car rolling)
- Decide how to roll the cars in a 'fair' way.
- Which do you think is the best roller?
- How do you think we could test your predictions?
  (Which rolls the furthest; which bumps into a wall 3m away?)
- How do we make the test fair?
  (Roll several cars down the ramp, start them at the top, just let them go, don't push them)
- How shall we measure how far they go?
  (From the end of the ramp, to the part of the car furthest away.)

NB Most of the cars will not go straight, but for this investigation, it will give a reasonable indication if you and the children measure from the end of the ramp straight to the front of the car, with a metre rule or a tape measure.

Individual and group work

The children use Sheets 1 to 4 to help them prepare, then do their tests. Encourage the children to test each car more than once, discuss any big differences in the measurements, then test it a third time if necessary. They record their results on Sheets 2 to 4.

Whole class

Discuss the results:

● Which were the best rollers?

● How far did the best/the worst roll?

● How did you make the test a fair one?

● What problems did you have?

● What did you do about it?

● Whose prediction was right?

● Why did this car go the furthest/shortest distance? (the wheels, the size)

Reinforce the major skills and ideas — testing from the same starting point, problems with swerving cars, making the test fair.

● Whose car do you think was best overall? (If there's time, investigate to reinforce the learning from the first tests.)

Differentiated Sc1 learning outcomes

Suggesting a question to test and predict what will happen

● from exploration, suggests which might be the best roller

● suggests a question — Which is the best roller?

● suggests a testable question. Which will roll the furthest? Which will roll the straightest?

● from a selection of cars, makes a prediction — I think this will roll the furthest.

Planning

● makes suggestions about how to roll the cars

● makes suggestions about how to roll the cars in a 'fair' way

● suggests what measurements to take, such as 'measure from the end of the ramp to the front of the car'

● suggests what measurements to take if the path of the car is not straight.

Measuring

● with help, measures length in standard units

● measures in centimetres and metres

● repeats a measurement.

Recording

● records measurements in a simple, prepared, table

● records measurements and comparisons in a prepared table

● with help, records predictions, comparisons and conclusions

● records predictions, comparisons and conclusions.

Concluding

● uses the results to make comparisons

● says whether their prediction was correct.

● explains the results simply — This is the best, it's got big wheels

● explains more scientifically — This one went the furthest because its wheels are straight/spin more easily.

Evaluating

● says whether they did the test in a fair way

● suggests/recognises that the path of the cars differed and might have affected the accuracy of measurement.

Using the differentiated sheets

Sheet 1★★ gives children practice in measuring length, height and distance. They may complete it with help where appropriate. (Measuring length, height and distance is a Level 2 activity. When using standard units in the course of an enquiry this corresponds to the Level 3 criteria in Sc1.)

Sheet 2★★ asks the children to write how they did their test, complete a simple table and use the results to decide which car rolled the furthest. (Level 2 activities.)

Sheet 3★★★ asks the children to make a more detailed record of the investigation, including how they made the test fair and asking them to explain the result. (Level 3 activities.)

Sheet 4★★★ asks the children to report on their planning, details of the test and measurements and to explain the result.(Level 3 activities.)

Sheet 5 is the sheet for recording children's skills in the enquiry. Some children will need help filling them in.

Background information

Predicting and raising questions

When the children are exploring how cars roll down a ramp and along the floor, they will begin to say which is the best way to roll the cars and which one they think is the best. These predictions are based on practical experience. They are a kind of 'educated guess', from which a question can arise and be tested scientifically:

Which car will roll the furthest? I think this one will. Why?

Planning

Exploring is a valuable prelude to this investigation. This will become clear to the children as they practice and repeat rolling the cars to find the best way to do it. They can then plan to do the test in as fair a way as possible.

Most children will see the need for measurement to answer their question but only a few, if any, will be conscious of the need for accuracy or to repeat their measurements. As the cars rarely roll in a straight line there is a built-in problem here, but the children can still make comparisons between the cars by measuring from the ramp to the car in a straight line.

Using the results

To young children, what they remember doing and what happened is more real than the numbers they recorded in their table. Interpreting figures and drawing conclusions from tables and charts is more difficult for them. Point out how the distances on the table matched what they saw happen and help them to draw conclusions using both sources of evidence.

Evaluating the test

Fairness is something that all children have a concept of. By this stage they will be developing understanding of a fair test so they will be in a position to say if they did the test fairly; that is, starting the cars in the same way from the same point on the same ramp. Their experience with the swerving cars will make children aware that they cannot always measure precisely the effects of varying one factor in an investigation. This presents us with a good opportunity to start children thinking about the reliability of their results.

Explaining the results

Children like to know why or how things are as they are and are often eager to suggest explanations for events and phenomena. They will have plenty of ideas to explain why (meaning 'what is the reason for') this car is the best roller: 'Because it's got good/large wheels', 'Because it's the heaviest'. These statements are, at this stage, explanation enough.

Cars rolling

As a car goes down a ramp, it accelerates; on reaching the floor, it decelerates and eventually comes to a stop.

Three factors which affect how far a car will roll are its weight/mass, the height of the ramp, and friction — due to the surfaces of the ramp and floor, and how freely the wheels move. (Friction is explored further in Year 4 Unit 5.)

A heavy car with good, big wheels will roll the furthest because:

- as it goes along the floor, the big wheels will experience less resistance on their spinning axles than smaller ones so it will not slow down so quickly

- its greater mass will prevent it from stopping as quickly as a less massive car as it has greater momentum.

Name .... Date ....

Which cars are the best rollers?

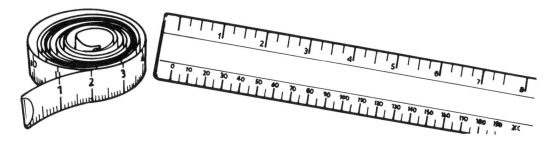

What can you use for measuring length, distance and how far a car rolls?

....

Measure these with a metre stick:

How high is your table?	m	cm
How high is the teacher's desk?	m	cm
Which is higher, your desk or the teacher's?		
How far is it across the corridor?	m	cm

Measure these with a tape measure:

How long is the window sill?	m	cm
What is the distance between your table and the door?	m	cm
What is the longest distance you measured?	m	cm
What is the shortest distance you measured?	m	cm

Name .... Date ....

Which car rolls the furthest?

What I did ....

....

....

My results

Car	How far it rolled		The longer distance
	1st time	2nd time	
1			
2			
3			
4			

Which car rolled the furthest? ....

Name .... Date ....

Which car rolls the furthest?

My prediction ....

I think this car will roll the furthest because ....

....

Here are my results:

Car	Distance it rolled		Notes
	1st time	2nd time	
1			
2			
3			
4			
5			

The car that rolled the furthest is ....

The car that went the shortest distance is ....

We made the test fair like this: ....

....

My prediction was ....

I think car .... rolled the furthest because ....

....

....

Name .... Date ....

Which car rolls the furthest?

We rolled cars
down a ramp
like this:

Which car did you think would roll the furthest? ....

We measured from ....
to .... with a ....

Results:

Car	Distance it rolled		Notes
	1st time	2nd time	
1			
2			
3			
4			
5			

Why did you measure them twice? ....

....

Which car rolled the furthest? ....

Was your prediction right? ....

Why is car .... the best roller? ....

....

Name .... Date ....

Which car rolls the furthest?

My planning skills

☐ I can help decide what to do.
(Level 2)

☐ I can decide what to measure.
(Level 2)

☐ I can see when the test is not fair and say why.
(Level 3)

My measuring and testing skills

☐ I can measure how far the cars roll by counting

.... (Level 2)

☐ I can measure how far the cars roll using a

.... (Level 3)

☐ I can carry out a fair test with some help.
(Level 3)

My concluding skills

☐ I can say whether my prediction was correct or not.
(Level 2)

☐ I can explain the results. (Level 3)